Original title:
The Mystery of Life's Directions

Copyright © 2025 Creative Arts Management OÜ
All rights reserved.

Author: Robert Ashford
ISBN HARDBACK: 978-1-80566-057-6
ISBN PAPERBACK: 978-1-80566-352-2

# Enigmas in the Fog

A cat in a hat walked quite askew,
Chasing its tail, just to see who knew.
The fog held secrets, they giggled and danced,
Whispering tales of a chance romance.

A shoe on a tree, a sock in a pond,
Who ties these knots? Oh, we're all quite fond.
We laugh at the puzzles we stumble upon,
While the universe chuckles, till the break of dawn.

## Gossamer Threads of Fate

A spider spins dreams on a whimsy thread,
While the mouse in the cupboard thinks, 'Oh, I'm fed!'
The clock strikes twelve, yet nothing is right,
As time does the tango with bats in the night.

Umbrellas fly high, but why do they care?
Mice wear tiny shoes, with no thought of a wearer.
We dance in the chaos, a jolly brigade,
While fortune just giggles, a waltz serenade.

## Riddles in the Wind

Through trees and the leaves, the secrets do sail,
A chicken plays checkers, quite ready to fail.
The wind whispers softly, yet how should it be?
Do we follow its whim, or is it the key?

Pinecones take bets on a squirrel's next leap,
While rabbits knit scarves, in a world half-asleep.
With every loud honk, a riddle unfurls,
Life's like a circus, with giggles and swirls.

## Threads of Yesterday

Yesterday's laughter has tangled in time,
With cats on stilts and a tree that can rhyme.
Pasta debates with a walnut and pen,
What is the score of this whimsical zen?

A giraffe wearing glasses, it aims for the moon,
While frogs play the banjo, in tune to a tune.
We weave all these threads, in a patchwork so bright,
Life's but a jest, in the glow of twilight.

## Labyrinths of the Heart

I wandered down a twisty lane,
Where feelings dance like a runaway train.
Love's map is drawn in crayon bright,
Yet I still trip in the soft moonlight.

Chasing hearts like butterflies,
I trip on shoes of huge size.
With every turn, a giggle escapes,
In this heart maze of silly shapes.

## Shadows of the Unknown Journey

I set out with a sandwich in hand,
Hoping to find some kind of land.
But shadows whispered tales so sly,
Even the squirrels gave me a side-eye.

Each corner turned, a rubber chicken,
In this quest, the fun was thickening.
With every step, I laugh and leap,
Questions like rabbits, they just won't keep.

## **Unseen Compass**

My compass spins like a dancing cat,
Leading me where? Just fancy that!
North? South? Or maybe a tea shop?
Every direction makes me stop.

With sticky notes and doodles galore,
I'm out exploring, but what's in store?
The path ahead is a silly tease,
I'll map it out with candy and cheese!

## Riddles of the Wandering Mind

In my head, a circus parade,
Thoughts that dance never evade.
Like clowns that juggle jellybeans,
Life's wacky puzzle is full of scenes.

I question it all with a quirky grin,
Why is it that I never win?
A riddle or two takes me for a ride,
In this playful maze where laughter must abide.

## Lanterns in the Fog

In the haze where shadows play,
Frogs wear hats and dance away.
A compass spins, lost in jest,
As I search for my missing vest.

Socks on trees and shoes in streams,
Map drawn in crayon, full of dreams.
A cat in glasses, reading a sign,
Whispers, "Hey, your path's divine!"

Jellybeans grow on sunlit trails,
Giggles erupt from tiny snails.
With every twist that I embrace,
I stumble on, a cheerful race.

So bring your snacks, don't pack much pride,
We'll wander wide, it's quite a ride!
With lanterns bright and laughter loud,
We'll puzzle out this happy crowd.

## An Odyssey of the Mind

In a realm where thought's a comet,
Ideas fly, a drumming sonnet.
I trip on clouds, fall through the sky,
And wonder why do picky pies cry?

Chickens debate in silly stores,
While socks hold court on kitchen floors.
The toaster sings a rebel tune,
As I chase thoughts like butterflies in June.

With brainwaves dancing like a ballet,
I misplace keys in the light of day.
A pickle whispers, so profound,
"Your path is lost where fun is found!"

So grab a jester, plot a course,
We'll dodge the rants, seek joy's resource.
An odyssey indeed, it's true,
But only if we let the silliness brew.

## **Whispers in the Twilight**

As dusk falls like a sleepy cat,
The fireflies chat, what's up with that?
A gopher drives a roly-poly car,
While wise old owls share thoughts bizarre.

The moon winks down, a playful tease,
While trees wear hats in the evening breeze.
A squirrel juggles, oh what a sight,
In whispers soft, they plot the night.

Bubbles float from the flowers' song,
Chasing thoughts that never last long.
As laughter bounces off stars above,
They guide us with a gentle shove.

So wander on, past twinkling eyes,
With silly hearts beneath silly skies.
For in each wrinkle of dusk's soft glow,
Are laughs and giggles that help us grow.

## Labyrinths of the Heart

In mazes drawn with silly strings,
A heart may dance and sprout some wings.
With every turn, a chuckle found,
As my cat negotiates with a mound.

Balloons float by, they're on the run,
While toasters toast in warm, bright fun.
A jellyfish offers heart-shaped maps,
Twists of fate wrapped in giggle traps.

Through corridors where shadows grin,
I skip and hop, my heart a-din.
Each wrong way leads to laughter's cheer,
As ticklish secrets draw us near.

So take a step, don't fret the fray,
In labyrinths of joy, we play.
With every corner's silly turn,
Embrace the heart, let joy discern.

## The Mask of Tomorrow

Tomorrow wears a funny hat,
It jiggles when it laughs at that.
It points and giggles at my shoes,
As if they've got the latest news.

With shoes like those, I'll twist and shout,
Chasing rainbows roundabout.
Each step I take, a dance, a play,
Tomorrow's mask is here to stay.

## Metaphors on the Journey

On this road, I see a cat,
Wearing sunglasses, cheeky brat.
It winks at me while sipping tea,
Suggesting life's a comedy.

With every turn, a plot unfolds,
Like socks that giggle in the cold.
Just follow whims, let nonsense steer,
For metaphors are far and near.

## **The Secret Language of Pathways**

The paths I walk, they giggle loud,
Whisper secrets in the crowd.
A squirrel chats with a passing bee,
As if they've figured out the key.

Where do I go? The trees all grin,
They've seen the chaos, they've seen the spin.
I'll dance with fate, do the twist,
In this language that can't be missed.

## The Art of Following Instinct

My instincts sing like opera loud,
Wearing shoes that make me proud.
With each misstep, I laugh and cheer,
For every wrong turn steers me near.

Like a duck in a top hat, I waddle about,
Following instincts, without a doubt.
In this silliness, I find my way,
Navigating life's funny ballet.

## Shadows Beneath the Stars

In the dark, we twirl and spin,
Chasing shadows, let the fun begin!
Jumping puddles, socks all wet,
Finding treasures we can't forget.

Whispers from the laughing trees,
They surely hold the biggest keys.
A cat meows, just like a sage,
Guiding us through this great stage.

A lost shoe here, a hat goes there,
Who needs silence? We love the flair!
With echoes of giggles far and wide,
The stars are our friends, never to hide.

Under moonlight, we dance and roam,
Each corner feels a bit like home.
Mischief glows in the night's embrace,
Life is a wacky, wild race!

## Pathways Unseen

Two lefts and a right, I spin in place,
Running in circles, what a silly chase!
But then there's a squirrel, with a fancy hat,
Maybe he knows where the cheese is at!

Stumbling on pebbles, oh, what a fright,
Tripping over nothing, in broad daylight!
A giant balloon bobs, just out of reach,
What could it hold? Some lessons to teach?

A sign points left, but right seems fun,
Why follow rules when you can just run?
Riding breezes, laughing at fate,
Finding my path on this rollercoaster date!

The world spins round, a merry-go-trip,
With ice cream cones that occasionally slip.
In pathways unseen, we wander and play,
Lost in our laughter, come what may!

## **Echoes of Forgotten Dreams**

Once a dream whispered in my ear,
Like a rubber chicken, it danced with cheer!
I forgot my plan, but that's alright,
I'll follow the giggles through the night.

Echoes bounce off the pizza shop walls,
Where pickles hold meetings and the pizza calls.
We swing from wishes like we're on a slide,
Hoping that laughter stays by our side.

The burgers tell stories, the fries chime in,
In the carnival of thoughts where the fun begins.
Waving balloons, I stumble past fate,
Wishing on stars to lighten my plate.

Though dreams may fade like a misty fog,
I'll chase them down, just like a dog!
For in this dance, we find our schemes,
In echoes of laughter and forgotten dreams.

**The Compass of the Soul**

My compass spins, like a top on fire,
Telling me tales of my deepest desire.
With a giggle and grin, it points to the sky,
Who needs a map when you can just fly?

A pirate hat here, a treasure chest there,
The compass knows secrets hidden in air.
Finding joy in the most peculiar places,
With a hint of mischief, we throw silly faces.

My heart beats jazz while I follow its tune,
Chasing the moon beneath a sunny afternoon.
Between misplaced socks and a dancing shoe,
I'll wander the world, scouting the new!

So let's skip some stones and hop over logs,
Collecting sweet moments, like little frogs.
With each twist and turn, the laughter rolls,
Guided by light, thanks to my joyful soul!

## Searching for North

With a compass that points to the sky,
I wander and wonder, oh my oh my!
The map says go left, but I just feel right,
Lost in a forest, I dance with delight.

The trees all are laughing, they know where I stand,
But they'll never tell me, not even a strand.
I've asked every squirrel, the wise old owl too,
They just chuckle and say, 'How lost are you?'

## The Veil of Illusions

I peek through the curtain, it's all a big bluff,
They promise me answers but it's mostly just fluff.
Mirrors reflecting what's not even there,
I question my wardrobe—do I even wear air?

The shadows are dancing, they wiggle and sway,
I can't tell if it's night or it's merely the day.
A riddle, a puzzle, a laugh or a sigh,
Perhaps I'm just dreaming, or maybe I fly.

## Steps into the Unknown

I step with great caution on paths made of fog,
Where each little rock might just be a dog.
I trip over nonsense and leap over fears,
And giggle out loud as I wipe away tears.

The universe chuckles, it spins in a dance,
It offers me jellybeans, then says take a chance!
I follow the giggles, the whoops and the cheers,
What fun it is stumbling for countless light years!

## **Shimmers of Insight**

A glimmer, a flash, what was that little tease?
It tickles my thoughts like a gentle breeze.
I chase after sparkles, they shimmer and tease,
I grasp at their tails, and they slip with the ease.

The laughter of wisdom, it echoes so bright,
It twirls like a dancer in the soft moonlight.
I'll take all these lessons wrapped in a bow,
For who knows the answers? Just let's enjoy the show!

## **Footprints on the Shore**

Footsteps dance upon the sand,
Crabs and seagulls form a band.
Waves whisper secrets to the night,
While shells giggle, what a sight!

Every grain holds a tale untold,
Of socks and sandals, brave and bold.
Yet here I stand, lost at sea,
Was that a fish, or just me?

A lighthouse winks with a cheeky grin,
It's hard to know where to begin.
Do I follow the moon's bright path,
Or build a castle, feel the wrath?

Seagulls cackle as I trip,
With every slip, my wardrobe's grip.
Footprints fade but laughter stays,
As tides tease through silly ways.

## **Silent Signs of the Universe**

Stars twinkle with a wink and giggle,
While planets spin, doing the jiggle.
Signs that flicker in the vast abyss,
Tell me, is that a sign or a miss?

A comet zooms with a flashy flair,
While aliens wave and lose their hair.
Messages in bottles from outer space,
In glowy script, 'You're in the wrong place!'

The sun does yoga, stretching wide,
While the moon plays hide and seek, what a ride!
Do I chase the stars or grab a snack?
Cosmic paths seem to lack a track.

Yet laughter echoes in this cosmic play,
As I drift and twirl, come what may.
The universe chuckles, lights in a swirl,
So off I go, for another twirl.

**Clues in the Cosmos**

Puzzled faces look up at the sky,
Wondering where all the answers lie.
Asteroids dance like they've lost the beat,
While meteors crash with a comic retreat.

Galaxies swirl like a frosty cake,
I'm just here for a light-hearted break.
The Big Dipper pours coffee, oh-so-slick,
While Orion's Belt shows off his new trick.

A telescope peers with curious glee,
But is it finding clues or just a bee?
Constellations giggle, bright as can be,
As I chase shadows, mysterious and free.

Even black holes have a comedic side,
Swallowing stars with a laugh, not a guide.
Each clue I gather makes me smile wide,
In this cosmic riddle, I find my pride.

## The Hidden Map

A map drawn in crayon, what could it mean?
With scribbles and doodles, it's quite the scene.
X marks the spot, or so it claims,
But I found a dog instead, playing games.

Mountains upside down, rivers that dance,
Does this lead to treasure or just a chance?
The compass spins like a dizzy whirligig,
While I chase my shadow, feeling quite big.

The legends read of pirate lore,
But I trip o'er junk on my living room floor.
Can I find gold, or just some old shoes?
This map's a riddle, oh, what shall I choose?

Yet every line seems to lead to fun,
Adventures with laughter, life's number one.
The hidden map guides me with glee,
In the game of life, I'm always free!

## Navigating the Veils of Fate

A compass spins with glee,
Where am I meant to be?
The map is all a blur,
Do I follow the small fur?

Cats seem wise, I must obey,
As they lounge the day away.
With every twist, I take a turn,
For laughter is what I yearn.

Each path is paved with jigs and jives,
As squirrels plot their little lives.
I ask the birds for only hints,
They squawk and steal my breadcrumbs since.

So here I tread in joyful dance,
With every misstep, there's a chance.
If fate throws pies, I won't complain,
I'll wear a slice, and learn to feign.

## Curves of Consciousness

Life's a rollercoaster ride,
With loops and twists, I slide.
I try to keep my lunch inside,
But all the twists make it subside.

There's wisdom in the whoops and shrieks,
The joy is found quite in the peaks.
Around each bend, I shout with glee,
Is that a tree or is it me?

I search for signs in clouds of fluff,
But they just giggle, that's enough!
I'll follow rabbits, and maybe ducks,
But oh, the luck! It's all just luck.

So let the turns unfold like fate,
With all the quirks, it feels just great.
I'll take each curve with wide-eyed cheer,
Life's silly dance is oh so near!

## **Unraveled Threads of Time**

I knit a future, just for fun,
But dropped a stitch, oh what a run!
The yarn is tangled, a colorful mess,
Yet here I am, feeling quite blessed.

I tug on fate with gentle hands,
And chase my dreams like silly bands.
One thread leads me, then it's gone,
Hey, did I see a leprechaun?

With every twist, the clock does chime,
And I misplace my sense of rhyme.
But laughter echoes through my day,
Who needs a map? I'll make my way!

So let the chaos spin around,
In threads of joy, I'll be unbound.
For life is just a playful tease,
And I'll embrace it with a wheeze!

## Silent Signals in the Stillness

In quiet moments, I eavesdrop,
On squirrels plotting, oh they hop!
A flicker here, a wiggle there,
Is that a sign, or just fresh air?

I glance at clouds and wonder why,
They seem to giggle, floating by.
Their shapes shift quick—a dragon, a shoe,
Life's a riddle I'm meant to chew.

The ground beneath begins to hum,
It might just be a tuba's thrum.
I dance to rhythms, soft yet strange,
Each silent cue feels like a range.

So in stillness, I take my cue,
From signposts only dogs pursue.
For in the quiet, laughs abound,
A silly life is often found!

## The Journey Unknown

With maps that make no sense at all,
We wander paths, we stumble, we stall.
A compass spins, it plays a game,
The road ahead is never the same.

In pizza shops, we seek our fate,
Should we turn left or just tempt fate?
Life's a riddle, a jester's jest,
And every turn's a wild, fun quest.

The signs we see are pure confusion,
As if planned by a prankster's illusion.
Yet laughter guides us down this lane,
And joy returns, again and again.

So here we roam, with laughter loud,
In a world that's silly, endlessly proud.
With every bump and twist divine,
We share a grin over the wine.

## Secrets Beneath the Surface

In ponds of croaking frogs and flies,
Lie secrets wrapped in deep disguise.
We dip our toes, but where's the depth?
Is it just mud, or something we prepped?

Squirrels plot their daring schemes,
While we chase down outlandish dreams.
Is there a prize, a secret prize?
Or just a nap beneath the skies?

As treasure maps lead us astray,
We dance along, come what may.
The truth's a joker in this play,
With butterflies that steal the day.

A game of hide-and-seek we find,
With every riddle left behind.
So laugh with me at shapes we draw,
And swim through wonders with our awe.

## Navigating Uncharted Waters

With rubber ducks on a cardboard boat,
We sail the seas, footloose and remote.
The ocean's wild, with waves of cheese,
And jellyfish that tickle our knees.

Oh, seagulls squawk their fashioned lore,
As we chart a course for 'who knows what's more?'
With treasures marked on a silly map,
We risk it all for a giant flap.

The fish parade in colors bright,
Dancing along with all their might.
Is that a shark? Or just my friend?
Around each wave, new fun to fend!

From pirate tales to mermaid songs,
Our laughter's where the heart belongs.
So raise your glass, and cheers to the crew,
In waters strange, we're brave and true.

## **Tides of Time and Space**

As clocks tick-tock and time takes flight,
We chase our tails into the night.
With spacemen wearing goofy grins,
We spin around, where chaos begins.

Each second's filled with silly sights,
Like gnomes in capes and silly lights.
The universe is quite the show,
With fish in hats and squirrels in tow.

We laugh at puzzling constellations,
While mapping out our strange foundations.
With every star, a wink or two,
They giggle back, as if they knew.

So times may shift, and tides may sway,
But we'll keep finding fun each day.
In this cosmic dance, we take the chance,
To twirl through life in a joyful prance.

## Foraging Through the Fog

In a world quite hazy and bright,
I'm lost as a cat in the night.
With a sandwich in hand, I set out,
Dodging birds that chirp and shout.

The trees all giggle, as I veer,
Did I mention I can't see clear?
My map is a doodle, what a sight!
Just follow the biscuits, it feels right!

A squirrel mocks my every turn,
As I pant and wheeze, it's my turn.
With each step, another surprise,
Like twinkling stars in furry skies.

If I trip on a root, will it cry?
Do the mushrooms plot? Oh, my, oh my!
With laughter and luck, I shall go,
In search of the cheese, never slow!

## The Unfolding Map of Existence

I unfolded a map with great flair,
But wait—this is just my grocery fare!
Looking for donuts, lost in a trance,
Got sidetracked by a dancing pants!

Rabbits hop in cocoa streams,
Chasing my ever-elusive dreams.
Each point plotted is quite absurd,
Is that a land of flying birds?

Navigating a world with a wink,
Found a treasure, or was it a sink?
Directions, they twist and they twirl,
Like a hula hoop in a playful whirl!

Chasing my shadow, it leads the way,
This whimsical dance brightens my day.
So here's to the paths that confound,
Where laughter appears, magic's found!

## In Quest of the Hidden Trail

I set off in search of a path,
With snacks in my pocket, right after a bath.
A signpost points, but they're all a joke,
Is that a bear, or just my smoke?

Through fields of socks and colorful shoes,
I stumble upon a herd of moose.
"Which way to the treasure?" I shout,
They lift their heads and all laugh out!

Behind each bush lurks a cheeky gnome,
With a wink, says, "You're far from home!"
Spinning in circles, I heed not their plight,
Until I trip on a gopher's delight!

But through the giggles and hints so sly,
I find a map where no one can lie.
Maybe the quest is just to embrace,
All the fun in this silly race!

## **Reflections on a Starlit Walk**

Under the stars, I roam so free,
But what's that noise? Is it just me?
With shadows playing peekaboo,
I'm here to find a taco or two!

The moon giggles at my wild chase,
As I trip over a frowning vase.
A raccoon steals my dreams, oh dear,
But who knew they wanted tacos near?

My thoughts chase fireflies, so quick,
With every zap, a brand-new trick.
Footprints lead to who knows where,
Is that the munchkin's house over there?

So I wander through night's cozy embrace,
Each corner brings a smile to my face.
With laughter and snacks, I put doubt to rest,
In this starry quest, I am truly blessed!

## Dreams of the Wanderer

In a land where socks go to hide,
A map made of pizza guides my stride.
I chased a cat who wore a hat,
Turns out it was my own pet rat.

I stumbled upon a dancing tree,
It swayed and giggled, 'Come join me!'
With every twist, I lost my shoes,
Now barefoot, I must choose my blues.

A talking rock gave me a treat,
Said, 'Travel light, or rest your feet!'
But then it rolled, off down a hill,
Now I'm chasing it, against my will.

A starry night with a moon that winks,
Offers sage advice—don't overthink.
With laughter echoing through the night,
I wonder where I'll sleep tonight!

## Over the Next Ridge

With each step I hear a loud clatter,
Is it a deer or my lunch platter?
I search for treasure, not gold or gems,
Just hoping to find some old rusty hems.

In the distance, a llama appeared,
Wearing sunglasses, it seemed rather weird.
'This is my turf, so please don't creep,'
But it smiled as I nearly lost my leap.

Over hills where the wild grass chokes,
I found a band of singing folks.
They strummed on ukuleles made of cheese,
An unexpected concert, brought me to my knees.

The sunset wrapped me in a glow,
As I danced with shadows in a shaky row.
With giggles rising into the air,
I dropped my compass, but I didn't care!

# In the Company of Shadows

My shadow's named Fred, he jokes a lot,
Together we ponder, 'What have we got?'
While the sun laughs, and the moon pretends,
We argue where the giggling goes when it bends.

Beneath the old oak, we take a seat,
Fred claims he's got rhythm, but can't find the beat.
With a wiggle and jiggle, I join in the fun,
We both laugh hard till the day is done.

We talk to the clouds, they giggle with glee,
'We float above you, come join us for tea!'
But as I reach out, they puff away fast,
Leaving me with a shade and a bit of a blast.

In twilight's embrace, we concoct a plan,
To dance with the fireflies, oh so grand.
With each little flicker, we set the stage,
In the end, it's laughs that truly engage!

## The Call of the Wild

A whispering breeze fills the air with cheer,
'Follow the river, it's wild and clear!'
With a swimming pool made of glittering dew,
I'd rather dive in than the neighbor's shoe.

I met a squirrel with bright red shoes,
Dancing around, saying, 'You can't lose!'
Join my parade of the utterly strange,
Where nonsense reigns and life's a big change.

Beneath a sky of cotton candy bright,
I questioned a cloud, 'What's your delight?'
It replied with a giggle, 'It's pie on my mind,'
Now I'm running, no pastry I find.

But as night falls, I'll sit and reflect,
On all of the joy that I didn't expect.
With wild dreams racing, I seem to recall,
That laughter is king, and it conquers all!

## **Whims of the Clouds**

Clouds dance like they're in a show,
Bumping into each other below.
One floats south; the other says, 'No!'
They're just lost, putting on a row.

Raindrops join in, saying, 'Let's play!'
They splash down in a cheeky way.
Umbrellas pop like mushrooms spry,
As giggles rise with every spry.

Sunshine peers with a wink and grin,
'Where's my coffee? The fun begins!'
Clouds gather round in a bubble cheer,
While birds shout, 'Hey, the coast is clear!'

A kite strings up in playful fights,
Twirling under the funny lights.
The winds are jesters in this game,
And nobody leaves without a name.

## Beyond the Horizon

Beyond the edge where the sea does play,
Swimmers get lost in a breezy ballet.
Mermaids giggle, pulling them deep,
While seagulls squawk, 'You can't win sleep!'

Pirates sail with a treasure map,
Turns out it's just a big ol' gap.
They stop for tea, forget the gold,
'Even Scrooge needs warmth -so I'm told!'

In the distance, a sunburnt whale,
Winks at a sailor with a windy tail.
'You think you're lost but I'm just bored,
Let's swap tall tales; I'm truly floored!'

As night falls, the stars come out,
Giving directions without a doubt.
But those big bright lights start to tease,
'You need glasses! You can't be pleased!'

# The Unfolding Journey

A snail set off on a grand trek,
With a thought bubble; 'What the heck!'
Slow and steady, it had its dreams,
While ants passed by with hurried schemes.

It stopped to snack on a leaf that's green,
While butterflies laughed, 'You're not mean!'
It replied, 'At least I've got my pace,
No traffic jams in this slow race!'

Beneath a mushroom, it took a break,
Asked a frog, 'What's this whole mistake?'
The frog croaked back, 'Enjoy the ride,
Every step taken adds to the pride!'

And when the sun set the ground aglow,
The snail grinned wide at what it could show.
Life's about giggles and squishy trails,
And the wondrous tales that time unveils.

## **Paths Through the Wilderness**

In the dense woods where the critters stroll,
A raccoon says, 'Hey, isn't this bold?'
Squirrels argue 'bout who took the nut,
While a wise owl thinks it's all a glut.

Branches wave as if they're saying, 'Hi!'
They tap a tree, it whispers a sigh.
'Just follow your nose,' the flowers insist,
But bees buzz loud, adding to the twist.

Footprints lead down the wrong way round,
Lost in laughter, not a frown found.
A deer tips its hat, 'Are you lost, my friend?'
The raccoon grinned, 'Ah, this fun won't end!'

With a wink to the moon, they danced at night,
Forgotten paths are a laugh-filled fright.
For every a detour brings a new cheer,
In the wild where folks shed a funny tear.

## Winding Pathways of the Soul

In a maze of silly turns, not quite right,
My compass spins, yet I still feel light.
A banana peel leads to a hidden door,
I trip and stumble, but always want more.

Round the corner, a squirrel in a hat,
It waves at me with a jaunty chat.
I follow its lead to a fountain of pies,
Where all my worries just flutter and fly.

With each hop, I'm lost, but having a ball,
Dancing with shadows that mock and enthrall.
Life's wobbly edges are cozy and bright,
Every misstep a reason to laugh with delight.

So let's roll on this pathway, not straight at all,
With giggles and grins, we'll answer the call.
Who knew that confusion could be such a ride?
On these winding pathways, let joy be our guide.

## Secrets Beneath the Surface

Underwater giggles bubble through seas,
Where fish don top hats and dance with ease.
The depth holds secrets, some silly, some grand,
A clam tells jokes while juggling on sand.

Bubbles float up, twisting into a dance,
Mystical mermaids invite you to prance.
They whisper of treasures but playfully pout,
Saying, "Just one more joke, before we head out!"

Swirls of kelp sway like a funny old tune,
I wave to a turtle, my aquatic cartoon.
Finding the surface is all quite absurd,
With giggles and gags lost within every word.

So dive deep into laughter, let worries all flee,
The ocean's a circus, come swim wild and free.
What's down in the deep? Oh, it's surely a laugh,
In the secrets beneath, find joy's hidden path.

# Echoes of the Uncharted Road

Stumbling along with a map upside down,
I bump into bushes, oh what a clown!
The path is a riddle that none can disclose,
But I carry my snacks, so I'm never too close.

Every fork in the road has a sign that's a joke,
"Detour for dancing, avoid all the yoke!"
I waltz with a cactus, its spines all aglow,
In this charming confusion, I relish the flow.

Little creatures join in—what a quirky parade,
A raccoon wearing glasses in bright, dazzling shades.
Every echo I hear has a smile on its face,
As I meander gently through this joyful place.

The road may be wild, and the signs may bemuse,
But laughter is plenty when you don't have to choose.
So here's to the echoes that tickle the soul,
On the uncharted road, let humor take hold!

## Whispers in the Twilight

In the dusk when the shadows all start to sway,
A cat in a tutu leads waltzing ballet.
The stars pop out with a giggling glow,
And fireflies flicker, putting on a show.

"Follow me!" calls a voice with a husky old twist,
A raccoon chef claims there's nothing you missed.
He offers odd dishes, like moonlight soufflé,
Each bite brings a chuckle, a hearty hooray!

The night is alive with peculiar delight,
Every whispering breeze takes a chance to unite.
Here's to the moments that seem out of place,
In the twilight's embrace, we all find our grace.

So let's frolic through night, with laughter's sweet tune,
Under the shine of a welcoming moon.
In the echoes of whispers, let joy brightly beam,
For life's little quirks are the heart of the dream.

## The Dance of Choices Unseen

In the ballroom of my mind, I twirl,
Dancing with decisions, I give a whirl.
Left is a laugh, and right goes a sigh,
Each step like a puzzle, oh my, oh my!

Should I wear that hat or go without?
The mirror giggles, it has its clout.
My shoe's on my left but my sock's on my right,
What choices are these in this waltz of delight?

The cat gives a stare, judging my groove,
I trip on the rug; it's all a smooth move.
The chips are on me, the stakes have been raised,
With every misstep, I'm utterly fazed!

But oh, what a journey, this dance has begun,
With chuckles and stumbles, just look at us run!
In the end, it's a riot, a whimsical spree,
Life's a funny dance, come twirl along with me!

## Beneath the Canopy of Questions

Underneath the branches where thoughts play tag,
Questions hang like fruit on a colorful rag.
Should I leap high or stay on the ground?
Witty whispers surround, a riddle profound.

The birds chirp gossip, "What's your next quest?"
I say, "I don't know, but I'll give it my best!"
Should I chase after clouds, or stay put for rain?
You know, life's a circus, with joy and with pain.

A squirrel scolds me, "Quit pondering much!"
While I chase my own tail, just look at the touch!
The grass tickles my toes, as I ponder the sun,
In this playground of wonders, I'm never quite done.

But who needs a map when the sky's so wide?
With giggles and jesting, I'll sway with the tide.
Each leaf tells a story, each breeze holds a clue,
Dancing beneath questions—oh, what should I do?

## Waypoints in a Dream

In a land of bizarre, where socks find their mates,
I chart out my path with some rather odd states.
Perhaps I'll go left to the land of lost keys,
Or traipse to the right, where I'll converse with bees.

With a map made of candy, I tack on some spice,
Each waypoint a whimsy, oh, isn't it nice?
The compass spins wildly, it points in all ways,
And the stars smile down, offering sassy displays.

With a wink and a jig, I hop on a cloud,
While telling the sun, "You're just way too loud!"
The moon gives a shrug, "I'll light up your flight,"
And the comets say, "Join us, we'll party all night!"

Yet somewhere in laughter, I stumble and slip,
My dream's like a surfboard; what a wild trip!
But isn't it grand, this whimsical scheme?
Floating through waypoints, lost in a dream.

## Fleeting Moments of Clarity

A fog rolls in thick, where thoughts like to play,
But then comes a spark, brightening the gray.
Like a flash in my mind, it darts to and fro,
"Why did I just eat the last slice on show?"

In moments so fleeting, I find hidden gold,
Why chicken is fried and why socks get so old?
Answers dance by like butterflies swift,
But just as I grab them, they shimmer and drift.

I attempt to record them, but paper's a tease,
When I write down the thought, it merely will freeze.
"Why's the fridge empty?" I giggle aloud,
Perhaps it's a secret, I'm still not allowed!

Yet in those bright flashes, there's humor displayed,
In this mad quest for meaning, it seems I've mislaid.
So here's to confusion, and laughter that flows,
In fleeting clarity, anything goes!

## Stars that Guide the Way

Twinkling lights up above me,
Winking like they know my name.
I ask them where to go next,
They giggle! Life's just a game.

Lost a shoe on the sidewalk,
Now I walk in a funny way.
Maybe I'll hop like a bunny,
Chasing stars that light the fray.

Question marks float in the sky,
Like clouds that forgot their cue.
I'll ride a comet to dinner,
If only my stars weren't so blue.

With a map made of candy,
I set out to find my way.
But I spilled it on the pavement,
Guess I'll just wing it today!

**Footsteps on the Edge of Tomorrow**


Tiptoe on the edge of dreams,
With one foot in yesterday's shoe.
A dance with a squirrel, perhaps,
Who says the dance won't come true?

Each step feels like a circus,
Juggling thoughts that flip and twirl.
I trip over my expectations,
And laugh as I see them swirl.

Future's like a wobbly chair,
Might tip over, might not stay.
I'll take a seat by the window,
And let the breeze lead the way.

With a lollipop compass in hand,
I'll navigate cotton candy clouds.
Adventure waits with a wink,
As the world laughs, giggles, and shrouds!

# Enigmas in the Breeze

Whispers in the rustling leaves,
What secrets do they conceal?
Maybe the wind is a prankster,
Steering my fate with a wheel.

I chase a butterfly giggling,
It flutters, just out of reach.
Like finding socks in the laundry,
Life's riddles are hard to teach.

Clouds form shapes of mischief,
An octopus on roller skates!
I ponder, as I sip my drink,
Are they handing out blind dates?

The sun's tickled by the clouds,
Who else but will join the fun?
I follow their lighthearted game,
And laugh as the day is spun!

## Signs Written in the Sand

Footprints leading to nowhere,
With squiggles like a toddler's art.
I wonder if they're telling me,
To just take it easy, start!

An arrow drawn by a crab,
Points to shells that dance and sing.
I'll follow the music of waves,
And join in the tide's silly fling.

Messages churn in the foam,
Like secrets that slip through my grasp.
I'll craft my own ones in the sand,
And let the ocean have a laugh.

As the tide washes all away,
I giggle at what's left behind.
For every sign that vanishes,
A new one's born – how divine!

## In Search of the Right Turn

I drove my car with zeal and flair,
But ended up in a llama fair.
With woolly beasts and folks askew,
I asked, 'Are you lost?' They said, 'Who knew!'

Google Maps said to take a left,
But I took a right, oh what a theft!
I ended up at a pickle rave,
Dancing with jars, feeling quite brave.

Should've packed a compass or two,
Or maybe just asked a kangaroo.
They seem to hop with such great ease,
While I'm still wondering where's my cheese!

So here I seek my own small gain,
In this wild world of joyful pain.
Each turn may twist, each laugh may spin,
But I'll cherish the madness from within.

# Reflections Along the Course

On a winding road, I hum a tune,
While squirrels negotiate the afternoon.
I waved to a sign that said 'Keep Right',
But it winked at me, oh what a sight!

A cafe beckoned with the best pie,
But GPS said, 'Just drive on by!'
So here I sit with my pastry plight,
Pondering if it's wrong or right.

Clouds drift lazily, so grand and wide,
Sometimes I just want to take a ride.
To nowhere at all, where laughter lives,
Where my car and I just spin and give.

Reflecting on roads both near and far,
The journey's twist beats being a star.
Every direction takes me in glee,
Who needs a map when you're wild and free?

## **Whispers of Forgotten Turns**

In a town where llamas roam at night,
I asked a toaster for directions, quite a sight!
It whispered soft, 'Toasty falls are near',
I giggled loud, for the end was clear.

Rounding corners in my old sedan,
I ponder life like a wobbly fan.
Got lost in thought, forgot my keys,
So now the squirrels are dodging fleas!

I stumbled on a sign that told me 'No',
But the laughter of trees urged me to go.
Next stop on this detour's delight,
A patch of daisies that danced in light.

Forgotten paths and giggles abound,
All the turns make a whirl of sound.
Embrace the whoops and the cheerful sways,
Life's playbook is a flurry of ways.

## Through the Veil of Uncertainty

A foggy morning, what's my quest?
A friendly snail said, 'You're the best!'
He pointed left, then right with glee,
But all I saw was a shiny bee.

Navigating through the misty haze,
My thoughts dance like a man in a blaze.
The path is tangled, full of quirks,
But laughter finds me where it lurks.

An owl gave wisdom wrapped in puns,
Claiming wisdom is for all the duns.
I nodded, then fell into a stream,
Life's directions are not what they seem.

So here I am, through veils I tread,
Each step a giggle, each turn a thread.
In this great riddle, where I belong,
I sing my strange but cheerful song.

## The Allure of the Unknown

In shadows dance the whispers old,
Where breadcrumbs lead and fortunes fold.
A squirrel maps a route with flair,
Chasing dreams in the vibrant air.

Upside down, the compass spins,
A treasure map, where none begins.
With every step, a goose might honk,
As life throws dice, we laugh and bonk.

A signpost reads: 'You've gone too far!'
Onward bound beneath a star.
Flip a coin, maybe heads, maybe tails,
Every journey has its funny trails.

So pack your bags and grab your cap,
For who knows, there's fun in the flap!
With one eye closed and a wink so sly,
We'll strive blindly and give it a try.

## The Canvas of Choices

Brush in hand, we paint with glee,
Splatters of choices, oh what a spree!
Colors clash in a splendid fight,
As left and right entwine in sight.

Each stroke a question, plopped with flair,
This canvas could use a lot more hair!
Mix up blues with a dash of pink,
Then wonder how we'll eat and think.

Should I wear socks, or just flip-flops?
A little dance, and the music stops!
With every choice, a giggle follows,
As logic fades, and whimsy swallows.

So take a brush, make it a blast,
Life's quirks make the moments last.
In a world of colors, stand up and cheer,
For choices are messy, and that's the deal!

## **Beyond the Edge of Reason**

They say to think, but I don't care,
I'll ride a turtle, let's catch some air!
Logic snoozes behind a soft wall,
While I'm busy planning a mud-ball brawl.

Cows hold court in a field of dreams,
Beneath a sky that bursts at the seams.
Who needs rules when ducks do waddle?
They've got their own crazy cattle-saddle!

Here's to the maps drawn in crayon,
With routes that lead to a land of don.
With each twist, a giggle blooms bright,
As we prance around in pure delight.

So come join me on this laugh-out-loud,
Beyond all sense, we'll make it proud.
Reason may sleep, but I'll take my chance,
For life's a jumble with a silly dance!

**Each Turn a Story**

With every turn, new tales unfold,
Like rubber chickens, bright and bold.
A path that zigzags like a snake,
In search of fish-shaped cake to bake.

Every corner has a giggle, I swear,
From talking trees to flying chairs.
Who needs maps, or signs in the night?
When every step blooms pure delight!

So lend me your ear for the zany yarn,
From a dog who plays in fields of yarn.
A sprightly hop and a happy shout,
Each twist a story we can't live without!

At times it's wild, at times it's weird,
But laugh along, for that's what we cleared.
With whimsy's guide, let's find our way,
In this raucous tale of a fun-filled day!

## Fragments of Epiphany

A chicken crossed the road, oh dear,
To chase a thought, or was it a beer?
The light bulb flickers, bright with glee,
Did it find a path, or just take a pee?

In a world of choices, he scratches his head,
With options aplenty, should he stay or tread?
A signpost laughing, a wink in its eye,
"Turn left for trouble, or right for pie!"

He spins in circles, like a dizzy fan,
Trying to follow a curious plan.
But life's a riddle, not quite a game,
Each twist and turn feels just the same!

So dance on the path, let humor reign,
For wisdom often wears a silly chain.
In fragments of thought, we stumble and sway,
Finding joy in chaos, come what may!

## Shadows of Tomorrow

A shadow creeps with a giggle and wig,
Dancing on pavement, feeling quite big.
It whispers secrets, but can't keep a straight face,
Tomorrow's plans seem more like a race.

A cat on a fence looks down with a grin,
As it ponders the leap—will it fly or swim?
The shadow just chuckles, 'You've got this, mate!'
But what lies ahead? Oh, that's up to fate!

With maps drawn in crayon, the future's unclear,
"Take a left at the goose, then ride with a deer!"
Oh, how the plots twist, like pretzels in knots,
Navigating life's jests, not just the thoughts.

So grab your shadow, hold on tight,
Together you'll wander from day into night.
In the humor of life, we float and we glide,
And shadows of tomorrow become one wild ride!

# The Unseen Path

There's a path all unseen, like socks missing pairs,
Or keys held captive by elusive affairs.
With laughter a lantern, it lights up the way,
As you stumble along, come what may!

A squirrel in a top hat gives guidance supreme,
"Just follow your nose, it knows where to dream!"
He twirls with flair on the branches so green,
While you wander blindly, embracing the scene.

Around every corner, a riddle awaits,
Like why do we park on driveways? Strange fates!
With laughter and jest, confusion unfolds,
In the unseen path, adventure beholds.

So take off your shoes, let your toes feel the grass,
As you dance through the chaos, just let it all pass.
In the heartfelt giggles and moments that cling,
You'll find that joy is the funniest thing!

## Signs in the Sand

There are signs in the sand, but the tide won't wait,
A crab reads the future, but it's still late.
With arrows and symbols barely aligned,
'Clam chowder ahead!' is what the waves find.

A flip-flop stumbles, then does a jig,
Scribe warning notes, or dance like a pig!
The ocean chuckles, waves roll in and out,
In signs made of sand, there's a world full of doubt.

A message that says, "Watch out for gulls!"
In jest it is written, but who knows the pulls?
With laughter as lens, the signs are a game,
Drawn on a canvas that's never the same.

So sketch out your dreams, let the beach guide your fate,
With laughter big enough to dodge every bait.
In the signs of the sand, we shed all our woes,
Finding joy in the journey wherever life goes!

## Unknown Currents

Floating on a leaf in streams,
Where all my wildest wishful dreams.
The fish give me a sideways glance,
As if I've missed life's great dance.

I paddle hard with all my might,
In search of something just quite right.
But every bend brings puzzling sights,
Like ducks in hats holding flight.

With twists and turns I twist again,
Like tangled hair post-hurricane.
I ask the river, 'Where's the end?'
It chuckles back, 'Just around the bend!'

So here I float, with whimsy light,
On streams that giggle through the night.
Each ripple sings, a jester's song,
In currents where I can't go wrong.

## Stars That Guide

Winking stars up in the sky,
Teach me how to aim and fly.
One says 'left', another says 'right',
I trip on clouds, oh what a sight!

A comet waves with a glitter tail,
While I chase dreams that tend to fail.
Planets swirl, they spin and dance,
Beckoning me for my next chance.

'Choose a star!' they seem to shout,
But I can't tell what they're about.
A falling star, I take a swing,
And lose my grip on everything.

Yet here I am, a cosmic fool,
In this galaxy, I'm nobody's tool.
With cosmic jokes and twinkling pride,
The stars just laugh, and I'm their guide.

## Unwritten Chapters

Pages blank with lined delight,
Pens explode when dreams take flight.
I scribble plots and draw some lines,
But every twist just whines and whines.

Characters pop up, what a mess!
One's a cat in a polka dot dress!
Another yells, "What's next, my dear?"
I shrug and sip my floating beer.

Oh look, a twist! I make a plot,
But then they all choose to fight a lot.
A love triangle with a chair,
Just what I needed, life's cruel snare!

The book unfolds with giggles bright,
Yet I'm not sure who's wrong or right.
So I write on, no end in sight,
These chapters dance in pure delight!

## The Enchanted Road

A road appeared where none should be,
With singing stones and a dancing tree.
A squirrel dressed like a king,
Called out, "Oh traveler, try this thing!"

With cookies made of mushroom flair,
I took a bite, my feet in air!
The road kept changing, twist and twirl,
As goblins laughed and gave a whirl.

A sign that read, "Go left, go right!"
I spun around, it was quite a sight.
"Take the path with the fluffiest grass!"
But the road turned into a giant pass!

Yet off I went with giggles loud,
On this bewildering trail, so proud.
For every step on this odd route,
Is filled with joy, there's no dispute!

## Mesmerizing Detours

A twist and turn, oh what a ride,
Got lost in the park, but who needs pride?
The squirrels laugh, a comedic show,
I swear this path was here, you know!

Umbrella or key? A hat for my toes,
With breadcrumbs thrown, see where it goes.
The map's upside down, it's a total wreck,
Perhaps I'll just follow that guy on a deck!

An owl hoots softly, throws shade on my plan,
While I trip on a root, feeling like a man.
The moon winked at me, I gasped in delight,
Let's ditch the GPS; it's just not polite!

A path that zigzags, like a dancer on stage,
The trees all chuckle, they're wise to my age.
Who knew getting lost could be this much fun?
I'll bring snacks next time; it's a road well-run!

**Forks in the Road**

Two paths diverged, what a show,
One said 'Pizza,' the other 'No-go.'
I stood there scratching my head in glee,
When both options sounded good to me!

Left for dessert, right for the feast,
What's a hungry traveler to do at least?
With tummy grumbles and a wild cheer,
Flipped a coin, prayed it would steer!

Heard some birds gossiping high in the sky,
Talking 'bout detours, oh me, oh my!
Their beaks flapped tales of adventures galore,
And I chuckled, thinking, "I should explore!"

So I chose the fork that glimmered with fries,
Avoided the right, where excitement lies.
With each bite I took, with laughter it flowed,
The roads we choose brighten the load!

## Twilight's Secrets

Sun down, stars up, a riddle in light,
Where does the day go? It took off in flight!
A firefly mutters, "It's all just a game,
Play your cards right, forget about fame!"

I wandered in circles, felt dizzy and spry,
Chasing a shadow, or was it a pie?
Twilight chuckled, it blended the hues,
Mixed up my thoughts with its cheeky moves!

Should I follow the moon? Or that cat with a hat?
It winked and danced, now where's it at?
With giggles of stars, they twinkled with glee,
"Take a wild chance, go ahead, be free!"

So I twirled and I swayed in the twilight parade,
Finding secrets in laughter, as worries all fade.
Who knew this night would feel so alive?
Underneath playful skies, it's fun to just dive!

## The Dance of Decisions

In a swirling dance, my brain plays tricks,
Choices on the floor, all doing the mix.
A jig to the left, a salsa to the right,
I ask for a partner in the glow of the night.

Do I wear the red shoes or the blue shiny flats?
A disco ball spins, plays games like at bats.
As flavors of life blend in a twist,
I laugh at the silliness; forgot what I wished!

Step on a toe, oh, not a big deal,
Just a bump in the dance, keep the wheel.
Decisions all tangled like lights in a tree,
Letting the rhythm set pressure free!

From the waltz to the tango, I sway and I glide,
Decisions can cha-cha, in joy, I confide.
With silly little smiles, I laugh all the way,
For the dance of my choices is here to stay!

# Currents of the Unwritten Story

In an ocean of choices, I sailed my way,
With a map made of jelly, the sun led astray.
The compass spun wildly, as if it had fun,
Pointing left, then right, as I chased the sun.

I met a wise turtle, who chuckled with glee,
He said, "Take your time, it's all just a spree!"
So I danced on the waves, with a wink and a grin,
In the chaos of currents, it's a joy to begin.

The seagulls were laughing, squawking their song,
As I zigzagged my way, where do I belong?
But laughter is a treasure, a gold on the shore,
In the currents of chaos, there's always much more.

So here I sit, laughing, my journey unfolds,
With a quill made of feathers, and dreams to be told.
Life's book stays unwritten, a page yet to turn,
With ink made of giggles, I've nothing to yearn.

## Unfolding the Unseen

I peeked 'round the corner, what would I unearth?
A sock that went missing, it seemed to have worth!
It danced on the floor with flamboyant flair,
In this world of odd treasures, I'd better beware.

A banana peel whispered, 'You'll slip if you dare,'
While clocks ticked in whispers, giving me a scare.
The cat wore a top hat, and juggle he tried,
"Dance with the unknown!" was the cue he supplied.

The smell of fresh muffins wafted on high,
While shadows did tango, beneath the blue sky.
A wink from the squirrel, a nudge from the breeze,
In this land of the quirky, I felt so at ease.

With a laugh and a twirl, I embraced the bizarre,
In the unfolding of wonders, I'll reach for the stars.
For life's silly secrets are gilded with fun,
In the whimsical dance, we're all just begun!

## Celestial Clues Along the Path

With stars that were blinking, trying to chat,
I followed their giggles, 'Hey, where's my hat?'
The moon gave a wink, illuminating the way,
As I tripped on a comet, bright as the day.

Planets played peek-a-boo, in their cosmic guise,
"Catch us if you can," they teased with bright eyes.
I jumped on the Milky Way, like a cosmic slide,
Laughter echoed in space, as giggles would guide.

The sun threw a party with rays all aglow,
Where suns danced with planets, and comets put on a show.
I twirled with the asteroids, each spin was a cheer,
In the protons of laughter, all worries disappear.

So here in this wonder, the universe plays,
In celestial clues, I'm lost in a daze.
With humor as fuel, my heart takes the lead,
In the vastness of space, I'm no longer in need.

## **Tangles of Time and Space**

Time stretches and bends as I skip on a line,
A rollercoaster ride through the years, quite divine.
Tangled in moments, I twirl round and round,
In a whirlwind of laughter, new adventures I've found.

With clocks that go backward and calendars wild,
I'm a child of the cosmos, forever beguiled.
Yesterday's never and tomorrow's a game,
In this twist of the cosmos, who could feel shame?

An octopus juggled with jellybeans bright,
While time turned to pudding, all fuzzy and light.
I flipped through the pages of moments gone by,
With giggles and wiggles, I soared through the sky.

So cheers to the tangles, the knots that define,
With whimsy as glue, we embody the line.
In the circus of seconds, we dance and we play,
With laughter as our compass, life shows us the way.

## **Melodies of the Wandering Heart**

In the land where socks go astray,
A sandwich whispered, 'Come out and play!'
The sun wore shades, quite out of style,
While clouds danced cha-cha, oh what a smile!

A squirrel sang tunes from a tiny stage,
While dancing leaves flipped a gossip page.
The moon chuckled soft at a puzzled owl,
As stars debated which one to prowl.

A fish in the pond held court with a frog,
They plotted a heist on a wandering dog.
Laughter erupted as they shared their dreams,
A symphony played in starlit beams!

So here we roam, in this wiggly way,
With giggles and grins brightening the day.
For maps are for those who take life too keen,
We're the jesters here, living the unseen!

## Stars that Map Our Dreams

The stars took notes in a cosmic class,
While comets raced by, oh, what a gas!
A wishing star tripped on a cosmic line,
Slipping on stardust, it laughed, 'I'll be fine!'

Galaxies giggled, playing hide and seek,
While moons stacked marshmallows to peek and peek.
Constellations danced to a quirky beat,
As the universe whispered, 'Isn't this sweet?'

A cosmic chef stirred up dreams in a pot,
With sprinkles of laughter, oh, what a lot!
Planets exchanged tales from their distant shore,
While black holes pondered, 'What do we explore?'

So follow the stars, in all their glow,
With a wink and a smile, let your heart flow.
For dreams are the maps, quirky and bright,
Guiding our journeys through cosmic delight!

**Twists in Time's Threads**

In a clock that giggled, time took a turn,
With tick-tock tales for us all to learn.
A cat wore a hat, quite floppy and strange,
As seconds danced wildly, eager for change!

A turtle zoomed by, leaving trails that gleamed,
While seconds sipped tea, and apples all dreamed.
Moments did cartwheels, laughter in the air,
And clocks spun around in a silly affair!

The past had a party, invited the now,
With futures all giggling, 'We'll show you how!'
They played hopscotch on the threads of a weave,
Shouting, 'What fun it is to just believe!'

So here we glide, through moments so bright,
With twirls and swirls in the waltz of the night.
For time is a jester, that loves to unwind,
In every twist, joy's what we find!

www.ingramcontent.com/pod-product-compliance
Lightning Source LLC
Chambersburg PA
CBHW071846160426
43209CB00003B/430